This book belongs to:

....

The Secret Ballerina

Written by Nicola Baxter

Illustrated by Gill Cooper

ARMADILLO

Published by Armadillo Books
an imprint of Bookmart Limited
Registered Number 2372865
Trading as Bookmart Limited
Blaby Road   Wigston
Leicestershire   LE18 4SE

5 7 9 10 8 6 4

ISBN 1-84322-212-4

Produced for Bookmart Limited by
Nicola Baxter
PO Box 215   Framingham Earl
Norwich   NR14 7UR

Designer: Amanda Hawkes
Production designer: Amy Barton

Printed in China

Contents

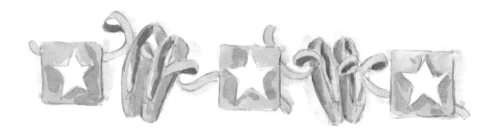

Holly's Ballet Class

Holly was grumbling. She often did. "I can't find the stupid thing anywhere," she moaned. "I don't see why I have to go anyway."

It was the usual fight before Holly's ballet lesson. She never could find her shoes and her tights and her costume and the bag she kept them in.

"We've got to go *now*, Holly," shouted her mother from the door. "Come on, Clara."

Little Clara appeared from her room, looking rather guilty. She was trailing Holly's leotard behind her.

"Give me that!" yelled Holly.

Usually at this time, Clara was playing with her friend Jonno next door, but he had chicken pox.

Mum, Holly and Clara arrived at ballet class five minutes after it had started. As Holly struggled into her tights, Mrs Mathilde, who was the teacher, glared at Holly's mother across the room. She didn't like her girls to be late.

"*When* you're ready, Holly," she said crisply. "Now girls, one, two, three!"

Holly's mother pressed her lips together and turned to hang up the clothes that Holly had dropped on the floor in her haste to get ready. There wasn't really time to go home and back before she had to pick Holly up again, so she usually dashed down the road to do a bit of shopping and maybe have a coffee. Today, though, she had Clara with her. Sometimes it was hard to dash with her younger daughter. Clara liked to stop and look at things. Well, perhaps they could just go to the café and have a drink instead.

"Come on, Clara," said her mum.

Clara didn't move.

"Now, Clara!" A little louder this time.

Clara was staring at the class at the other end of the big hall.

"I said *now!*" yelled Mum, and received another glare from Mrs Mathilde.

Mum went red in the face and grabbed Clara's hand. The little girl's feet hardly touched the floor as they hurried outside.

Mum helped Clara fasten her seat belt. It was only when she straightened up that she saw little tears streaming down her small daughter's face.

"What's the matter?" she asked. "Is it too tight?"

"I wanted to see the dancing," sobbed Clara.

Her mum frowned. Clara hardly ever cried. She was usually a calm and happy child. Mum put a hand on her forehead. Maybe she was getting one of the colds that were going around. Or Jonno's chicken pox. But Clara felt fine.

"We can't stay and watch, Clara," she explained. "Mrs Mathilde thinks the girls can't concentrate with mums there. But at the last lesson of term we can stop and see the lesson. You can come with me then, if you like. It's only a couple of weeks away."

Clara nodded but still looked sad. A couple of weeks seemed a long time.

Mum and Clara drove down the road to the shopping centre and went into the café. Mum bought Clara a cookie with sweets on it to cheer her up.

"This is nice, isn't it?" said Mum. "When we've finished, we'll go into the bookshop next door and see if we can find a little present for Jonno. Something about diggers, maybe. He'd like that, and he must be fed up having to stay at home."

The bookshop was not very busy, but it still took a long while to find the right book for Jonno. Clara knew which books he already had, so she was able to help Mum choose.

"Stay there," said Mum, "while I go and pay. I won't be a minute."

But when Mum came back, there was no sign of Clara. Mum panicked and started dashing round the shop, until she suddenly tripped, dropping her bag and her shopping! A little girl she knew quite well was sitting with her legs stretched out on the floor, concentrating so hard on a book she was holding that she hadn't even noticed her mum falling over her.

"Honestly, Clara…," Mum began, but she stopped when she saw Clara's face. It was really shining with happiness.

"Can I have this book, *please?*" she asked. "I'll make my bed for ever and ever and ever."

It was a book on ballet, and something made Clara's mum feel that just for once she simply couldn't say no.

Clara's Ballet Class

The next day, which was Saturday, Mum and Holly hardly saw Clara. She shut herself in her room. It was only by the thudding on the floor that Mum guessed she was looking at her ballet book and trying out some of the movements. Mum was impressed. Clara had only just started to learn to read, but she was trying very hard to understand some of the words in the book. Luckily, there were lots of pictures, too.

Upstairs in her room, Clara didn't notice when it was lunchtime or suppertime. Mum had to shout and send Holly to bang on the door.

"I can't come. I'm dancing," came a little voice from inside.

"It's not real dancing," scoffed Holly. "You have to go to lessons, like me. And anyway, it's not that great. The teacher is always telling you off. It's impossible to think about what your feet are doing *and* what your head is doing *and* what your arms are doing *and* listen to the music. A little girl like you couldn't possibly do it."

Thud! The noise from inside the room showed that Clara was going to try, however small she was.

When Clara finally appeared for supper, Holly nearly fell off her chair laughing. Clara had put on her swimming costume and tied a scarf round her waist. She had scraped back her hair and put a band round it, but it looked a bit spiky and odd.

"You're walking funny, too!" giggled Holly, as Clara moved round the table, with her back very straight and her chin up. Clara found her slippers by the back door and changed into those, too.

Clara didn't care. She sat very tall in her chair as she ate, but Mum frowned as she looked across the table at her younger daughter.

"Clara, sit still!" she said. "What are you wiggling about for?"

Holly looked under the table and laughed again. "She's dancing with her feet even though she's sitting down, Mum!"

"No dancing at the table!" said Mum, and then they all laughed because it sounded a bit strange.

After supper, Clara went back to her room. It was better now, because it was dark outside, and the big window near her bed made a wonderful mirror. She could see herself as she practised her foot positions.

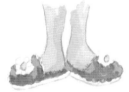 

First position…   second position…   third position…

fourth position…   and fifth position. Ooops!

None of them was easy. But Clara practised and practised until she didn't have to look at the book all the time. There was still quite a bit of thudding to be heard down in the kitchen.

"Bathtime, Clara!" called Mum, and Clara was about to protest when she had an idea and scampered off to run her bath. Mum sent Holly up to supervise.

"*Ouch!*" cried poor Holly as she came into the door. Clara's foot had just made contact with the squidgiest part of her tummy!

Holly saw at once what was happening. Clara had realized that the towel rail would make a perfect *barre* for her ballet practice. Holly laughed again, but she gave her sister a little bit of help, as well. She was keen to show that she knew a lot more about ballet than Clara – although to Holly's surprise, Clara did seem to find some quite complicated movements easy.

Mum thought that Clara would get fed up with her new interest in a day or two, but it didn't happen. Early on Friday, Clara started her campaign.

"Couldn't I go to ballet class, Mum?"

"Darling, you are too little," said Mum. "When you're bigger, we'll think about it. But it's expensive, and you'll be tired of it in a week. Besides, you'd need to be in a younger class than Holly, and I can't spend all afternoon running backwards and forwards with one or other of you. You can go and play with Jonno as usual. He's much better now."

Clara pleaded. She cried. She even stamped her feet and sat down on the front doormat when it was time to go. But Mum had made up her mind. Clara was delivered next door, and Holly, grumbling as usual, went off in the car.

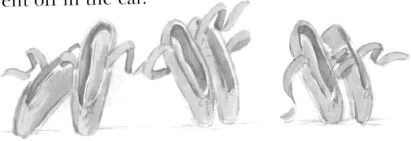

Jonno wanted to play with his tractors and diggers. Usually, Clara thought that was quite a good game, especially if they could scoop up mud from the garden and hide it in Jonno's slippers. But today, Clara had other things on her mind.

When he put his head round the door to ask if they would like juice and a biscuit, Jonno's dad was surprised to see both children twirling around the floor to one of Jonno's nursery rhyme tapes.

"Dancing?" asked Jonno's dad.

"Ballaay, Dad," called Jonno, breathlessly. "It's good. Look!" And he did a big jump that Clara had shown him and neatly swept all the books off a nearby shelf.

Jonno's dad took a deep breath and said, "I've got an idea. I'll be back in a minute."

Five minutes later, Clara and Jonno, with their drinks beside them, were watching a video that Jonno's dad had found. It showed a performance of a ballet called *The Nutcracker*. To Clara, it was magical, especially as the heroine shared her name!

The Disastrous Ballet Class

The following week, Clara could hardly wait until Friday. It was the day when all the mums and little ones could stay and watch their sisters dancing. Clara hadn't stopped practising all week except to watch the video that she had managed to borrow from Jonno's dad.

"Ugh, I know that boring thing," said Holly, making a face. "We're doing a bit of it in class. It's horrible. None of us can get it right."

At last it was time for Holly's ballet lesson. Clara had made sure to find all the things her sister needed in plenty of time, so that *nothing* would hold them up.

At the hall, Clara could hardly stand still, she was so excited. All the mums and little ones sat on chairs up on the stage at one end of the big room, while the girls in their pink leotards lined up in front of Mrs Mathilde below. Mrs Mathilde gave a fierce look at some of the mums who were whispering, then faced the class.

"Now, girls," she said, "today I want you to dance as you have never danced before, for we have a very special visitor." She waved her hand towards a small lady dressed in pink and white who was sitting at the side of the hall. "This, as some of you may know," announced Mrs Mathilde, "is Marcia Gray, a very famous ballerina indeed. She has recently bought a holiday home in our town, and we are truly honoured to have her with us today. Girls, please!"

Some of the girls who had heard of Marcia Gray were sighing and shuffling, although Holly just looked bored. Miss Gray smiled at the class and said, "Please, don't let me delay you. Carry on just as usual." She paid great attention to the class as it began, but Clara's mother noticed the visitor's eyes kept turning to the audience on the stage.

Clara watched the class with great interest, but she found that she kept meeting the eyes of Marcia Gray, too. Clara wasn't sure, but she thought she recognized her face. Surely she was the ballerina dancing the Sugar Plum Fairy on Clara's favourite video?

The class went on as usual. Mrs Mathilde tried to be charming but she was, if anything, even more tense than usual with the eyes of a great dancer upon her.

She snapped at the piano player and spoke sharply to the girls when they didn't listen to the music or follow instructions. Clara couldn't help noticing that

Holly really wasn't very interested in what she was doing, and, of course, that made Mrs Mathilde even more cross.

The end of the lesson was meant to be the performance of a little part of *The Nutcracker* that the girls had been practising.

"We are hoping to present this at our Christmas Show," said Mrs Mathilde, "but, naturally, it does need a good deal more work. The part of Clara, in particular, has yet to be cast. I have asked several girls to try the part today."

Marcia Gray nodded graciously. "I have been lucky enough to perform in this ballet many times myself," she said. "It is always a pleasure to see young people discovering it for themselves."

To be honest, what followed was not a great pleasure. The girls were clearly not comfortable in their roles. Mrs Mathilde grew more and more stressed, until she became quite hysterical as she shouted and hissed instructions at her dancers. Holly disgraced herself by colliding with another girl, who banged her leg sharply on the *barre* and had to be helped from the room by her mother. Holly's mother sank down in her chair and pretended not to be there.

Only Clara really enjoyed the performance, and she wasn't looking at the dancing at all. As the music began, she shut her eyes and saw in her head the perfect performance she knew so well. She didn't realize she was smiling.

Somehow, the class struggled through to the end of the piece. Marcia Gray clapped politely with the other members of the audience, but Mrs Mathilde went to pieces completely. She was almost in tears as she apologized to the visitor for the shambles she had just seen. "We should not have attempted it," she moaned. "I was wrong even to ask this class to try. And on your first visit, too. It's a disaster!"

Marcia Gray stood up and took control without seeming to make any effort at all.

"Nonsense, my dear," she said kindly but firmly. "It was a good idea to try, and really, I saw many good things in the performance. The problem is that you haven't found your Clara yet, and without a centre, the dance cannot hold together."

Mrs Mathilde sniffed. "But no one…," she began.

"Luckily," smiled Marcia Gray, "you have someone here who will perform the role beautifully. She has a lot to learn still, but she is a dancer to her fingertips."

Mrs Mathilde was confused. "You mean you…?" she stammered.

The visitor laughed. "Good heavens, my dear, I am twenty years too old! No, I mean this little girl in the audience." And she pointed to Clara!

A Secret No More

Mrs Mathilde gasped. Clara's mum quickly sat up in her chair. Clara was wide-eyed as Marcia Gray stretched out her hand to help her from the stage.

"Yes," said the famous ballerina, "for two weeks now I have had the great pleasure of watching from my window as a little girl in a lighted bedroom practises her positions and her pirouettes. It has been a delight. I recognized her when I came in today."

"But she doesn't even come to class!" said Mrs Mathilde.

"Well, you must make the most of her while you can," said Marcia Gray. "I think you'll find that she will be going on to greater things before you know it."

Then Clara told the famous ballerina her name, and Marcia Gray laughed at the coincidence. "It's a pity you don't have a costume," she said, "so that you could dance for us now."

"But I do!" cried Clara, pulling off her dress. She was wearing her old swimsuit underneath! Then the whole class fell about laughing, and even Miss Gray had to hide a smile, but she soon called them to order and turned to the pianist.

"When you're ready," she said. And to Clara she whispered, "Just don't think about anything but the dance. You'll be fine."

But Clara wasn't worried. As the music began, all she wanted to do was dance … and she did.

Yes, Clara danced. She counted under her breath, concentrating hard. She kept her back straight. She kept her head up. She kept her mind on what she was doing. And she did it beautifully.

As the music swirled around the room, she didn't even notice that everyone else had stopped dancing. She was lost and happy.

The music came to the end. Clara dropped gracefully to the floor, as she had seen Marcia Gray do in the video.

There was silence in the room.

Then Clara looked up to find Mrs Mathilde bending over her. There were tears in the teacher's eyes as she helped Clara to her feet.

Then she smiled and looked up at Clara's mum. Her voice was not quite as stern as usual as she said, "You will be bringing Clara to class next week, I hope, Mrs James? Please be on time."

Clara's mum could only nod. She seemed to be having trouble with her eyes, too.

And Clara gave Mrs Mathilde a big hug, and her mum a big hug, and Marcia Gray a big hug, and even Holly a big hug. And then she went back to the car – dancing all the way.